DK findout!
Dinosaurs

Author: Andrea Mills

Consultant: Dr Darren Naish

Editor Olivia Stanford
Project art editor Joanne Clark
Senior editor Gill Pitts
Managing editor Laura Gilbert
Managing art editor Diane Peyton Jones
Picture research Surya Sarangi
Pre-production producer Nadine King
Producer Srijana Gurung
Art director Martin Wilson
Publisher Sarah Larter
Publishing director Sophie Mitchell

Educational consultant Jacqueline Harris

First published in Great Britain in 2016 by
Dorling Kindersley Limited
80 Strand, London, WC2R 0RL

Copyright © 2016 Dorling Kindersley Limited
A Penguin Random House Company
10 9 8 7 6 5 4 3 2 1
001–291665–July/2016

A CIP catalogue record for this book
is available from the British Library.
ISBN: 978-0-2413-3134-7

Printed and bound in China

A WORLD OF IDEAS:
SEE ALL THERE IS TO KNOW

www.dk.com

Contents

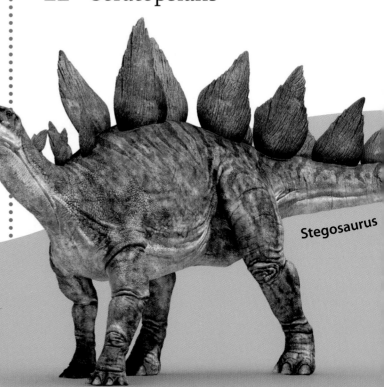

Stegosaurus

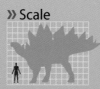

» Scale

The scale boxes throughout the book show you how big a dinosaur was compared to a person who is 1.8 m (6 ft) tall.

Pterodaustro

Sinosauropteryx

Sauropelta

Diplodocus

Triceratops

Tyrannosaurus rex

Teeth

Meat-eating dinosaurs, such as T. rex, had powerful jaws packed with huge teeth, ready to tear into flesh and bone.

Diplodocus

Neck

Feeding on the tallest treetops wa_ only possible for dinosaurs with very long, flexib_ necks, like the leaf-loving Diplodocus.

What is a dinosaur?

Millions of years ago, long before humans lived on Earth, a group of remarkable reptiles ruled the planet. Called dinosaurs, which means "terrible lizards", they all lived on land and had clawed hands and feet. However, some dinosaurs had long, pointed teeth, while others had thick, armoured skin, and some had feathers, just like birds today.

Iguanodon

Front limbs

Some dinosaurs had four sturdy legs for walking, while others had two arms and two legs. Iguanodon could walk on either two or four feet.

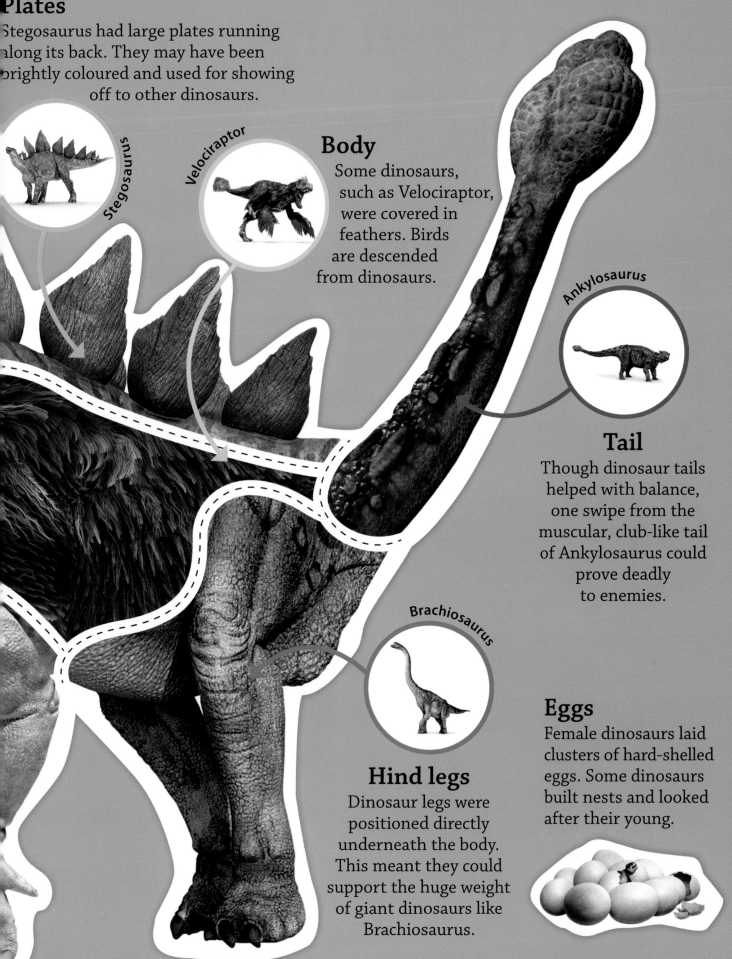

Plates

Stegosaurus had large plates running along its back. They may have been brightly coloured and used for showing off to other dinosaurs.

Stegosaurus

Velociraptor

Body

Some dinosaurs, such as Velociraptor, were covered in feathers. Birds are descended from dinosaurs.

Ankylosaurus

Tail

Though dinosaur tails helped with balance, one swipe from the muscular, club-like tail of Ankylosaurus could prove deadly to enemies.

Brachiosaurus

Hind legs

Dinosaur legs were positioned directly underneath the body. This meant they could support the huge weight of giant dinosaurs like Brachiosaurus.

Eggs

Female dinosaurs laid clusters of hard-shelled eggs. Some dinosaurs built nests and looked after their young.

Sizing them up

Dinosaurs have a reputation for being the biggest and fiercest creatures ever to inhabit this planet. While it is true that many were larger than a house, some were as small as a chicken. Scientific research has revealed the incredible range of sizes of these reptiles, and how each of the dinosaurs measured up.

Triceratops
Even though Triceratops was an average-sized dinosaur, it was still as long as two cars.

Sinosauropteryx
This little carnivore was a fast hunter, running on two feet. Sinosauropteryx grew to just 1 m (3 ft) long, which is about twice the size of a cat.

How do we know?

Dinosaurs died out 66 million years ago, so how do we know so much about them? Fortunately, scientists have found lots of dinosaur fossils, mainly of their bones. By examining their preserved bones and the tracks they left behind, experts can tell how large a dinosaur was, what it ate, how it lived, and even how it may have died.

95 million-year-old dinosaur bones

Looking at bones
Dinosaur experts take their finds back to the laboratory to find out more about them. The bones shown here are from a sauropod, a group of long-necked dinosaurs that were some of the biggest to ever walk the Earth.

Argentinosaurus

This super-sized dinosaur is one of the largest ever found. Argentinosaurus was as long as three buses and would have towered over a two-storey building.

Fossilized dinosaur footprints

Following in their footsteps

Scientists can learn a lot from dinosaur footprints. They reveal the dinosaur's size, whether it walked on two or four legs, the speed at which it was moving, and whether it was alone or travelling in a herd.

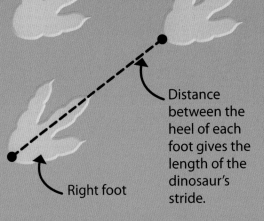

Distance between the heel of each foot gives the length of the dinosaur's stride.

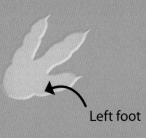

Left foot

Right foot

Dinosaur world

The Mesozoic Era is the name for the time when dinosaurs dominated the Earth. Lasting for over 180 million years, this enormous era is divided into three time periods called the Triassic, Jurassic, and Cretaceous. As the climate changed and new types of plants grew, different animals appeared. To describe when these periods were we shorten "million years ago" to MYA.

Jurassic period

The Jurassic period (201–145 MYA) saw changing seasons. A combination of high temperatures and rainfa[ll] caused flourishing fores[ts]. The lush vegetation included tall trees and widespread plants, providing a reliable food supply for huge plant-eating dinosaurs.

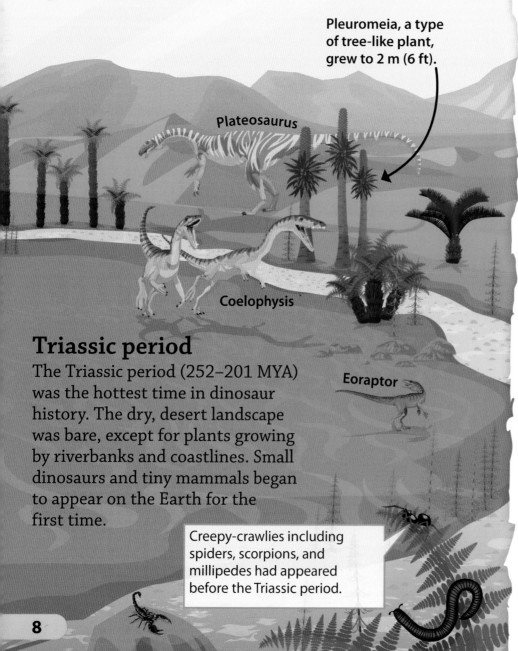

Pleuromeia, a type of tree-like plant, grew to 2 m (6 ft).

Plateosaurus

Coelophysis

Eoraptor

Triassic period

The Triassic period (252–201 MYA) was the hottest time in dinosaur history. The dry, desert landscape was bare, except for plants growing by riverbanks and coastlines. Small dinosaurs and tiny mammals began to appear on the Earth for the first time.

Creepy-crawlies including spiders, scorpions, and millipedes had appeared before the Triassic period.

Stegosaurus

Allosaurus

Insects like dragonflies and beetles flew through the air.

...erodactylus was
...lying reptile
...at lived in the
...rassic period.

Conifers, like this
monkey puzzle
tree, thrived.

Brachiosaurus

Cretaceous period

The final age of dinosaurs was the
Cretaceous period (145–66 MYA),
bringing a drop in temperature.
The warm and wet weather
produced rainforests and the first
flowers bloomed. Plant-eating
dinosaurs developed body armour
to protect themselves against the
fierce meat-eating dinosaurs.

Grass appeared
at the end of
the Cretaceous
period.

Tyrannosaurus rex

Triceratops

Many types of insect,
including bees, arrived.

Answer the questions to find out which group an individual dinosaur belongs to.

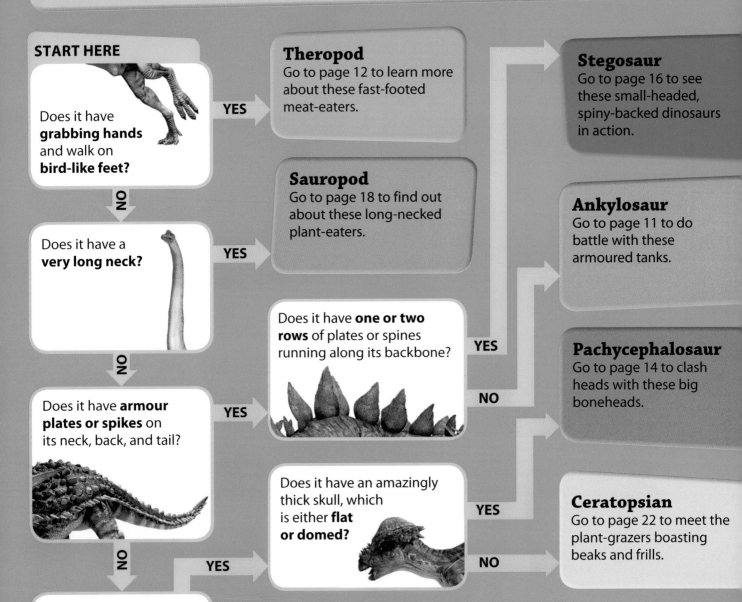

START HERE

Does it have **grabbing hands** and walk on **bird-like feet?**

YES → **Theropod**
Go to page 12 to learn more about these fast-footed meat-eaters.

NO ↓

Does it have a **very long neck?**

YES → **Sauropod**
Go to page 18 to find out about these long-necked plant-eaters.

NO ↓

Does it have **armour plates or spikes** on its neck, back, and tail?

YES → Does it have **one or two rows** of plates or spines running along its backbone?

YES → **Stegosaur**
Go to page 16 to see these small-headed, spiny-backed dinosaurs in action.

NO → **Ankylosaur**
Go to page 11 to do battle with these armoured tanks.

Does it have an amazingly thick skull, which is either **flat or domed?**

YES → **Pachycephalosaur**
Go to page 14 to clash heads with these big boneheads.

NO → **Ceratopsian**
Go to page 22 to meet the plant-grazers boasting beaks and frills.

NO ↓

Does it have an unusual head, with a **thick skull, a frill, or horns?**

YES → (to thick skull question)

NO ↓

Ornithopod
Go to page 20 to catch up with these agile plant-eaters.

Dinosaur detective

Dinosaurs come in all shapes and sizes, with many unique features. Experts have divided them into seven types, which share certain characteristics. When you know the difference, you can become a dinosaur detective and work out which one belongs to which group.

Giraffatitan

Long neck
to reach
tall trees.

Giant teeth

This terrifying 20 cm (8 in)
tooth belonged to T. rex. This
monster carnivore had huge
jaws, which contained up to
60 pointed teeth. They were
strong enough to bite clean
through bone and to tackle the
heavy armour of ankylosaurs
like Ankylosaurus. A bite
from a T. rex was 50
times more powerful
than a human's!

Pointed
tip and
serrated
edge.

! WOW!

Dinosaurs
continually **grew
and replaced** their
teeth throughout
their lives.

LIFE SIZE!

Carnivore teeth
were often
chipped and
damaged by use.

33

Hunting

Hunting in dinosaur times would have been a sight to behold. Meat-eaters used sharp claws and teeth to kill their victims. Sometimes packs of predators hunted together, combining their strength to bring down larger prey. Others hunted alone, relying on size and skill to take down their target.

Huge tail could be used as a powerful whip for defence.

At 13 m (43 ft) long, Giganotosaurus was larger than a T. rex.

Safety in numbers

Some plant-eating dinosaurs travelled in groups for protection. Together they could spot approaching predators more easily, like a herd of zebras might today. Predators find it harder to attack a large group because they need to single out a target.

Brachylophosaurus herd

ttle of the giants

hough Argentinosaurus was one of e biggest dinosaurs ever discovered, ganotosaurus could cause serious mage, especially to young or injured dividuals. It may have hunted in packs bring down larger adults.

Argentinosaurus was slow, meaning running away was not an option.

Serrated teeth were perfect for slicing through skin.

Theropod dinosaurs, like Giganotosaurus, ran quickly on two powerful back legs.

Colour

Fossilized bones cannot give us information about the colour of dinosaurs. However, throughout the animal kingdom, brightly coloured feathers or skin are known to instantly attract attention. Dinosaurs like Citipati may have showed off in the same way.

Frills

Meat-eating Cryolophosaurus didn't need a frill for protection. Instead, it is likely that its crest was brightly coloured and used for display. It may have appealed to females and scared away rivals. Many ceratopsians had fri for the same reason.

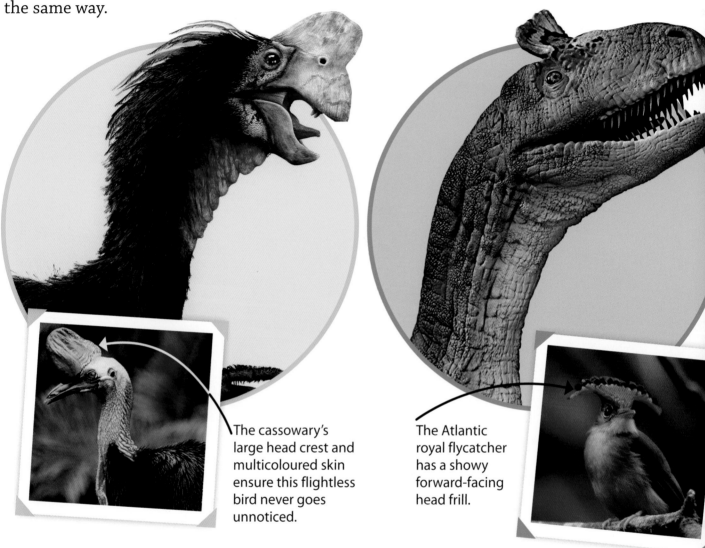

The cassowary's large head crest and multicoloured skin ensure this flightless bird never goes unnoticed.

The Atlantic royal flycatcher has a showy forward-facing head frill.

Showing off

In prehistoric times there was fierce competition to attract a mate, just like there is now. Dinosaurs developed special features to show themselves off to potential partners. Many millions of years later, animals today use similar tactics to stand out from the crowd and catch the eye of the opposite sex.

ose

ot much is known about dinosaur mating
lls, but Muttaburrasaurus might have
ed them to impress females. It had a
ny bump on its nose that may have had
 inflatable crest attached to it! This
uld have made its calls reverberate, so
ey were louder.

Horns

Prominent horns might have been used
as weapons when fighting rival dinosaurs
for females and territory. Like many
ceratopsians, Pentaceratops had long
brow horns that males may have
battled each other with.

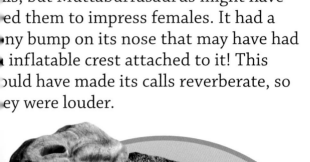

The elephant seal uses
its inflatable nose to
amplify its mating
roars, so they sound
even louder.

Male deer, called
stags, grow big
antlers to do battle
with rivals during
the mating season.

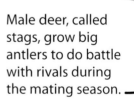

Male and female

The limited information about dinosaur
colour means we don't know if males and
females looked the same. However, lots of
male birds use a rainbow of colours to get a
female's attention. Male mallards, a type of
duck, have shiny green heads and purple
streaked wings in contrast with the duller
brown females.

Female and male mallards

Eggs

Like many of the dinosaurs themselves, eggs were often enormous. They were covered in hard shells like a chicken's egg, but were shaped differently. Although large, eggs were often much smaller than adult dinosaurs, so babies must have grown fast.

Citipati

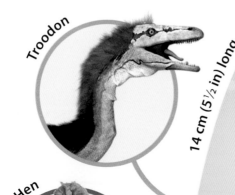

Troodon

Hen

18 cm (7 in) long

14 cm (5½ in) long

5 cm (2 in) long

Citipati egg
Fossil finds show that beaked Citipati laid at least 20 oval eggs in a nest. These eggs were as big as a human hand. Recent research has shown that Citipati eggs were a blue-green colour.

Troodon egg
Many fossilized Troodon eggs have been found. This meat-eating dinosaur may have laid as many as 24 eggs in a single nest, which were partly covered with plants to help keep them warm.

Chicken egg
Female chickens, or hens, lay small, hard-shelled eggs. They keep the eggs warm for about 21 days until the chick hatches.

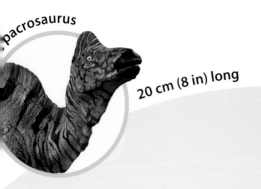

pacrosaurus

20 cm (8 in) long

Hypacrosaurus

The large eggs of plant-eating Hypacrosaurus were almost as big as a football. But even bigger dinosaur eggs have been found, which are more than twice the size of a Hypacrosaurus egg!

Nesting

Female dinosaurs often laid their eggs together in groups called clutches. Some made a nest covered in plant matter or earth for warmth, while others sat on the eggs and protected them. Some dinosaurs nested near each other for safety.

Hadrosaur nest

Inside an egg

In rare cases, the skeletons of unborn baby dinosaurs are found inside their fossilized eggs. This helps identify which dinosaur laid the eggs and gives an amazing chance to see what these babies would have looked like.

Hard shell
Shells were hard but broke easily, so newborns could break out.

Eyes
The unborn dinosaur's eyes were large, like the oversized eyes of many baby animals.

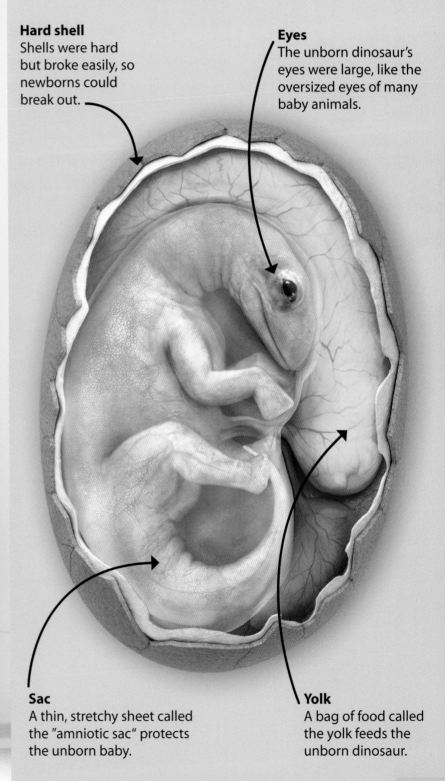

Sac
A thin, stretchy sheet called the "amniotic sac" protects the unborn baby.

Yolk
A bag of food called the yolk feeds the unborn dinosaur.

Parenting

Some dinosaurs were good parents, treating their eggs and babies with great care and attention. Fossils have shown that a few parents stayed with their eggs to keep them warm and to protect them against predators. When the eggs hatched, these dinosaurs fed and helped their young until they became able to look after themselves.

Staying safe

Today there are plenty of good parents in the animal kingdom. Crocodile mothers carry their babies from the nest to the safety of the water, while ostrich mothers and fathers watch over their chicks in a group, like children in a nursery.

A mother crocodile carefully holds a baby in her mouth.

Baby ostriches stay in a group for safety.

A baby Citipati would have used its beak to crack through its eggshell.

Citipati

In the 1990s this fossilized Citipati was found guarding its eggs, and was nicknamed "Big Mama". Its position is like a modern bird sitting on its eggs in a nest. Citipati was a feathered dinosaur and it may have been incubating its eggs, keeping them warm until they hatched. Later research has shown this dinosaur was probably the father, not the mother, of the eggs.

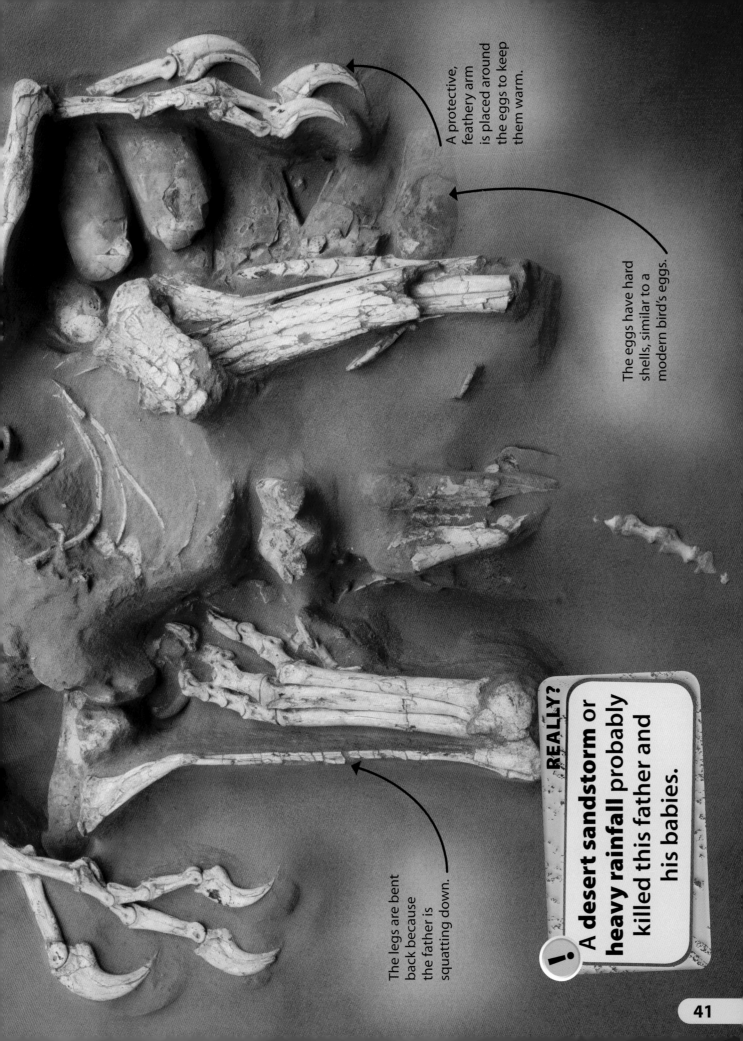

A protective, feathery arm is placed around the eggs to keep them warm.

The eggs have hard shells, similar to a modern bird's eggs.

The legs are bent back because the father is squatting down.

REALLY?

A desert sandstorm or heavy rainfall probably killed this father and his babies.

Baby dinosaurs

Remains of young dinosaurs reveal how babies grew and changed into adults. Like most young animals, baby dinosaurs had oversized heads, eyes, and feet until their bodies caught up in size. Although they started small, babies grew quickly and became fully grown dinosaurs in just a few years.

! WOW!

Maiasaura became the **first dinosaur in space** when bits of bone and shell were carried on a spaceflight in 1985.

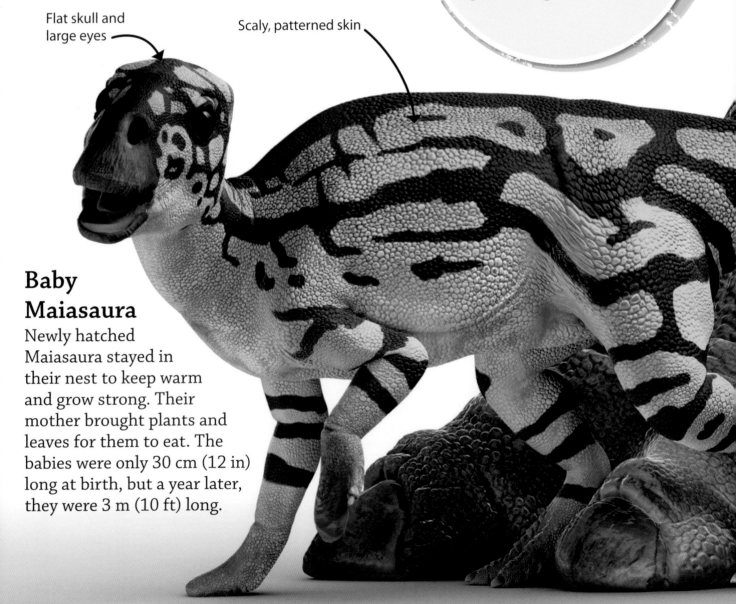

Flat skull and large eyes

Scaly, patterned skin

Baby Maiasaura

Newly hatched Maiasaura stayed in their nest to keep warm and grow strong. Their mother brought plants and leaves for them to eat. The babies were only 30 cm (12 in) long at birth, but a year later, they were 3 m (10 ft) long.

3 BABY DINOSAUR FACTS

1 The skeletons of some tiny newborn dinosaurs could fit in a human's hand.

2 Baby duck-billed dinosaurs, like Maiasaura, doubled in size in just six weeks.

3 Apatosaurus babies had to gain 14 kg (30 lb) of weight a day to reach their adult size of 18 tonnes (19.8 tons).

At 9 m (30 ft) long, the mother Maiasaura was the same length as a bus.

Maiasaura mother

Discoveries of the fossilized remains of adult Maiasaura next to hundreds of nests, eggs, and young show that the mothers looked after their babies. This is why this dinosaur was given the name Maiasaura, as it means "good mother lizard".

Growing up

The fossilized remains of large groups of Protoceratops have been found in deserts in Asia. The skulls show how their heads changed in shape and size as these dinosaurs grew up.

Hatchling skull
The skull of a baby Protoceratops shows the basic head shape, including the eye sockets and a tiny neck frill.

Juvenile skull
As Protoceratops starts to grow up, its beak gets longer, helping it to feed on plants.

Sub-adult skull
The cheeks have become wider and the beak more narrow. The neck frill is more developed.

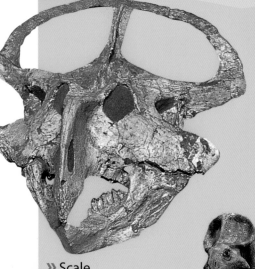

Adult skull
The fully grown Protoceratops skull has a strong neck frill and large cheek horns. Adults were about the size of a sheep.

» Scale

Adult Protoceratops

Feathers

Modern birds are the best known feathery animals. However, experts have found fossilized feathers, which proves that dinosaurs were feathered too. Dinosaurs developed feathers on their bodies for warmth, protection, and for display, a long time before they were used for flight.

A feathery crest may have attracted mates.

Velociraptor

In 2007, palaeontologists re-examined a Velociraptor fossil and discovered little bumps on its arm bones. The feathers of birds today sprout from similar bumps, called quill knobs, suggesting Velociraptor had long feathers on its arms.

Long feathers on arm.

Feather types

The first dinosaur feathers were simple structures like strands of hair. They provided warmth, attracted mates, and might have worked as camouflage, helping the dinosaur to hide. Over time, feathers developed into more complicated forms until they were ready for flight.

Hollow hair-like feather shape

Bristles
From scaly skin, dinosaurs like Heterodontosaurus grew basic hair-like feathers with a bristly texture. They were hollow, with nothing inside them.

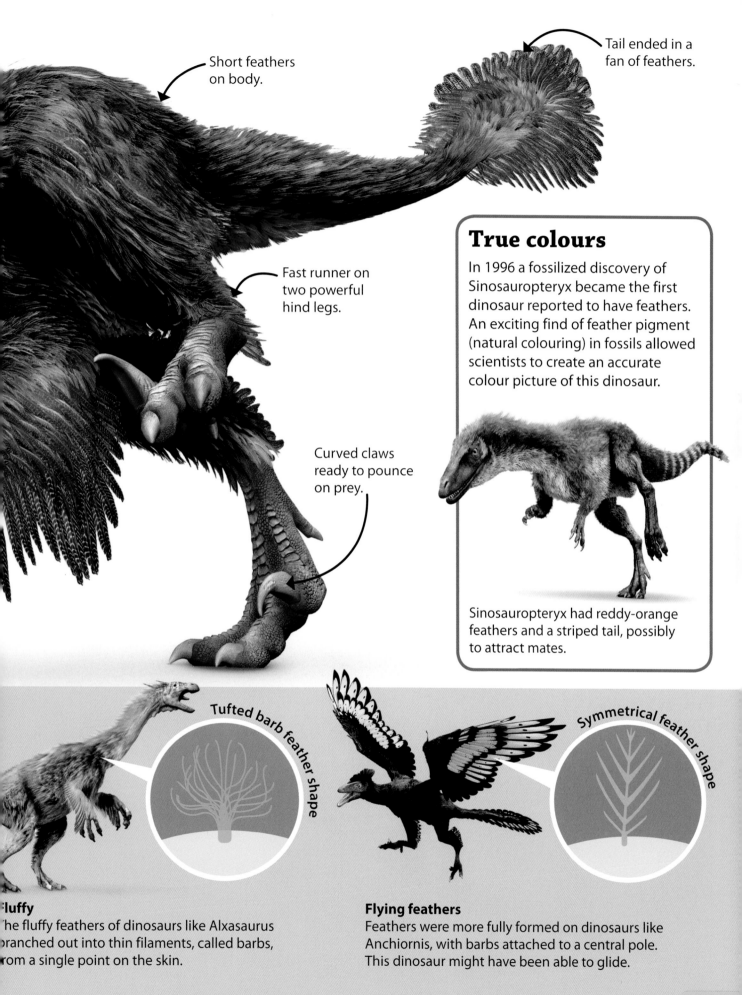

Short feathers on body.

Tail ended in a fan of feathers.

Fast runner on two powerful hind legs.

Curved claws ready to pounce on prey.

True colours

In 1996 a fossilized discovery of Sinosauropteryx became the first dinosaur reported to have feathers. An exciting find of feather pigment (natural colouring) in fossils allowed scientists to create an accurate colour picture of this dinosaur.

Sinosauropteryx had reddy-orange feathers and a striped tail, possibly to attract mates.

Tufted barb feather shape

Symmetrical feather shape

Fluffy
The fluffy feathers of dinosaurs like Alxasaurus branched out into thin filaments, called barbs, from a single point on the skin.

Flying feathers
Feathers were more fully formed on dinosaurs like Anchiornis, with barbs attached to a central pole. This dinosaur might have been able to glide.

Sea and sky

Dinosaurs stole the show in the prehistoric world, but they weren't the only reptiles around. Pterosaurs flew in the skies and sea-dwelling reptiles swam in the oceans. Marine reptiles included plesiosaurs, such as Albertonectes, and ichthyosaurs, such as Stenopterygius.

Its wingspan measured up to 1 m (3 ft).

Rhamphorhynchus

The flying Rhamphorhynchus took to the skies in the Jurassic period. This fish-eating reptile used its wings to soar over coasts and rivers hunting for prey.

Pointed teeth could hold tight to slippery squid.

Four flippers were used like paddles.

Albertonectes

This ocean swimmer had a neck longer than the rest of its body, with a record-breaking 76 neck bones. Flapping its flippers, Albertonectes could look along the seabed for shellfish or grab passing fish and squid.

Elasmosaurus

Long and lean, Elasmosaurus was a plesiosaur measuring around 9 m (30 ft). It swam slowly in the ocean, using its firm flippers to push itself through the water while hunting for fish.

...terodaustro

...his reptile lived and hunted by ...e beach. Pterodaustro was a ...ter feeder, scooping up water ... its big beak and straining ... to leave behind small ...a creatures.

A long, curved beak held about 1,000 teeth.

The large wings were well-adapted for flight.

Quetzalcoatlus

One of the largest animals to ever take flight, Quetzalcoatlus had a wingspan of 10 m (33 ft), the same as a small plane. It was about the same size as an adult giraffe.

The raised head crest might have been colourful.

The large wings were made of stretched skin.

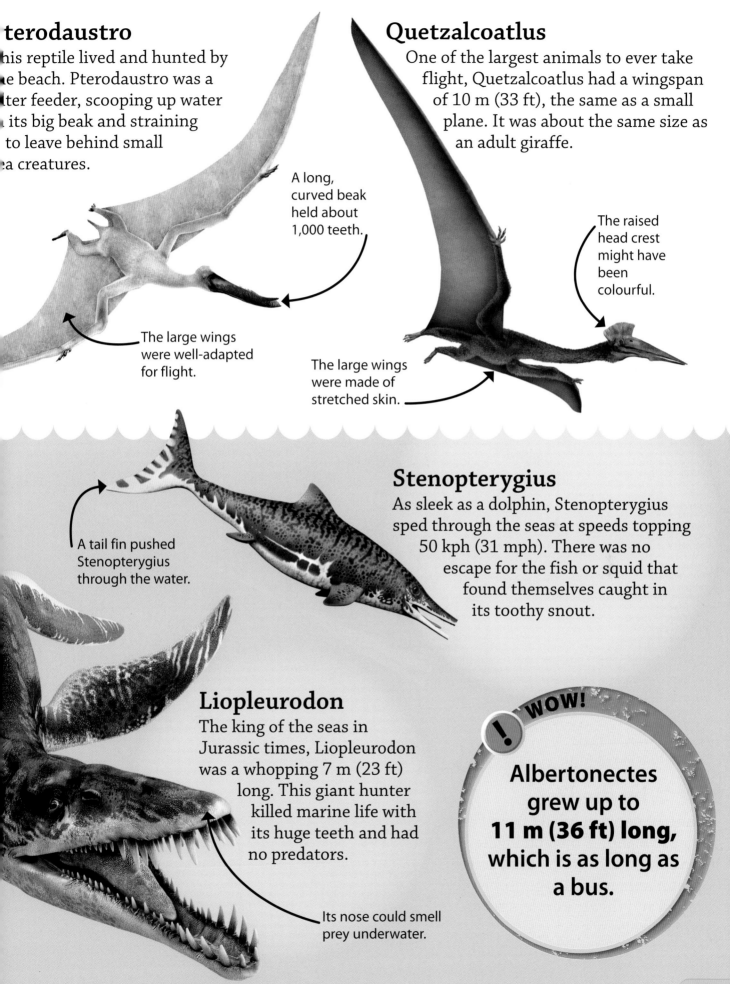

A tail fin pushed Stenopterygius through the water.

Stenopterygius

As sleek as a dolphin, Stenopterygius sped through the seas at speeds topping 50 kph (31 mph). There was no escape for the fish or squid that found themselves caught in its toothy snout.

Liopleurodon

The king of the seas in Jurassic times, Liopleurodon was a whopping 7 m (23 ft) long. This giant hunter killed marine life with its huge teeth and had no predators.

Its nose could smell prey underwater.

WOW!

Albertonectes grew up to **11 m (36 ft) long,** which is as long as a bus.

End of the dinosaurs

The age of the dinosaurs came to an explosive end 66 million years ago. Disaster struck when a huge rock from space smashed into planet Earth. At the same time massive volcanic eruptions released poisonous gases into the air. These events caused such an extreme change in the weather that many plants and animals died in one mass extinction.

Flying reptiles
Pterosaurs had ruled the skies for millions of years, but not one survived the extinction.

Dinosaurs
After 169 million years on Earth, the dinosaurs were wiped out in a very short space of time. They were badly affected by the cold temperatures.

Marine reptiles
None of the big reptiles that lived in the oceans survived the conditions after the meteorite hit.

Who died?
About 70 per cent of all life on Earth ended. No animal on land bigger than a dog survived the destruction. Fewer plants meant large herbivores starved and that meant less food for big carnivores.

Meteorite strikes!
Rocks from space that hit the Earth are called meteorites. Experts believe this meteorite measured a massive 10 km (6 miles) across. As well as killing nearby animals, the dust it caused stopped sunlight reaching the ground, causing the Earth to cool and plants to die.

Birds
Only 25 per cent of bird types survived the mass extinction. They are now the closest living relatives of dinosaurs.

Mammals
Most mammal groups managed to cling on during the extinction. They quickly took advantage of the disappearance of their dinosaur predators.

Invertebrates
Although many invertebrates were killed, the survivors bounced back. Today there are more invertebrates than any other type of animal.

Amphibians
Amphibians, like frogs, were lucky. It seems they were unaffected by the huge changes around them. Perhaps because they were small and could hide away.

Reptiles
Snakes, lizards, and turtles survived. Freshwater crocodiles were some of the largest survivors of the extinction in terms of size.

Who survived?
Some animal groups managed to adapt to the new conditions and we can still see their relatives today. With no dinosaurs to eat them, mammals grew to sizes they were never able to before.

Fish
Deep below the surface, smaller fish avoided the effects of the changes in weather.

Deinonychus

With its large, sharp claws and teeth, Deinonychus was a Cretaceous killer. This theropod dinosaur could run at high speeds and do a lot of damage with its weaponry. It is one of the dinosaurs most closely related to modern birds.

» **Length:** 3 m (10 ft)

» **Weight:** 80 kg (175 lb)

» **Diet:** Meat

» **Habitat:** Woodland

Two clawed feet were used for walking.

Sharp talons could rip flesh.

The small head crest may have been for display

Feathers covered Deinonychus.

Distant relatives

Chickens have dense feathers, which keep them warm and protect their skin.

You may not expect to see birds on a dinosaur's family tree, but they are their closest living relatives. In fact, birds are dinosaurs! During the Jurassic period, some meat-eating theropod dinosaurs developed into feathered fliers and although many of these birds died out in the mass extinction, some survived and have been flying high ever since.

toothless, horny
beak replaced the
terrifying teeth.

Large crest
attracts mates.

Stepping stones

Dinosaurs and birds may look completely different, but small changes over millions of years have had some big effects. Feathered dinosaurs took many different forms before becoming the birds we recognize today.

Short,
feathered
wings

Archaeopteryx
Alive in the Jurassic, one of the earliest bird-like dinosaurs was Archaeopteryx. It had the head, clawed hands, and tail of a dinosaur, but the wings of a bird. These wings were too weak for anything more than brief flight.

Long tail
feathers

Confuciusornis
By Cretaceous times, dinosaurs like Confuciusornis were even more like modern birds. The teeth and tail had gone, replaced by a toothless beak and flapping wings, though flying still proved challenging.

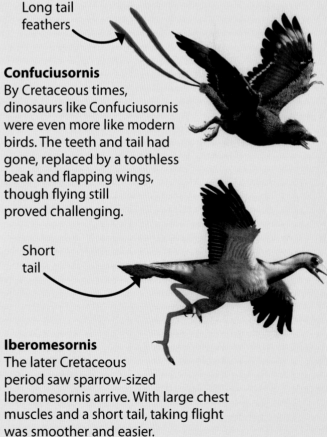

Short
tail

Iberomesornis
The later Cretaceous period saw sparrow-sized Iberomesornis arrive. With large chest muscles and a short tail, taking flight was smoother and easier.

FACT FILE

Chicken

Like all birds, chickens are the descendants of dinosaurs. These small birds share many of the features passed on from their giant ancestors, including feathered bodies, clawed feet, light bones, and hard-shelled eggs.

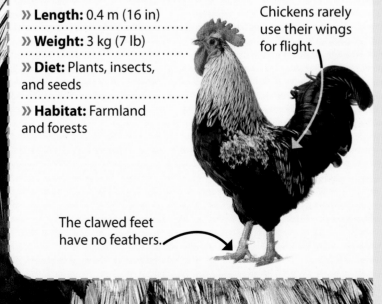

» **Length:** 0.4 m (16 in)

» **Weight:** 3 kg (7 lb)

» **Diet:** Plants, insects, and seeds

» **Habitat:** Farmland and forests

Chickens rarely use their wings for flight.

The clawed feet have no feathers.

New dinosaurs

Although they died at least 66 million years ago, new dinosaurs are still being discovered all the time. Once a fossil has been dug up, scientists need to check it and see if it should be named as a new type of dinosaur, which might take years. Who knows what odd fossil finds are yet to be made!

The fossilized skull of Aquilops fits in a human hand.

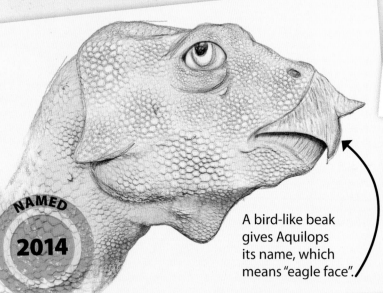

NAMED
2014

A bird-like beak gives Aquilops its name, which means "eagle face".

Aquilops

A skull the size of a rabbit's turned out be the earliest ceratopsian from North America. Aquilops was a four-legged plant-eater from the Cretaceous period with a strange spike on its nose.

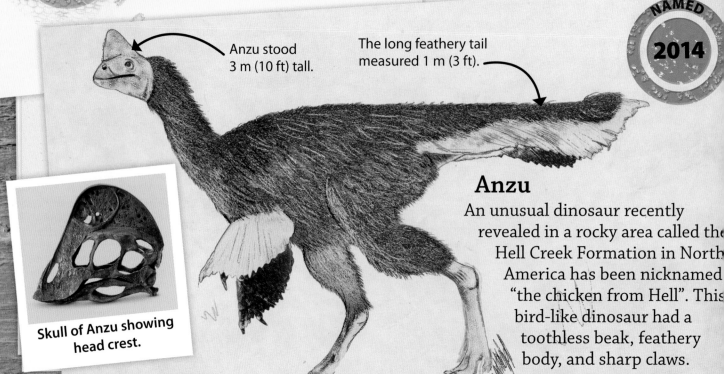

Anzu stood 3 m (10 ft) tall.

The long feathery tail measured 1 m (3 ft).

NAMED
2014

Skull of Anzu showing head crest.

Anzu

An unusual dinosaur recently revealed in a rocky area called the Hell Creek Formation in North America has been nicknamed "the chicken from Hell". This bird-like dinosaur had a toothless beak, feathery body, and sharp claws.

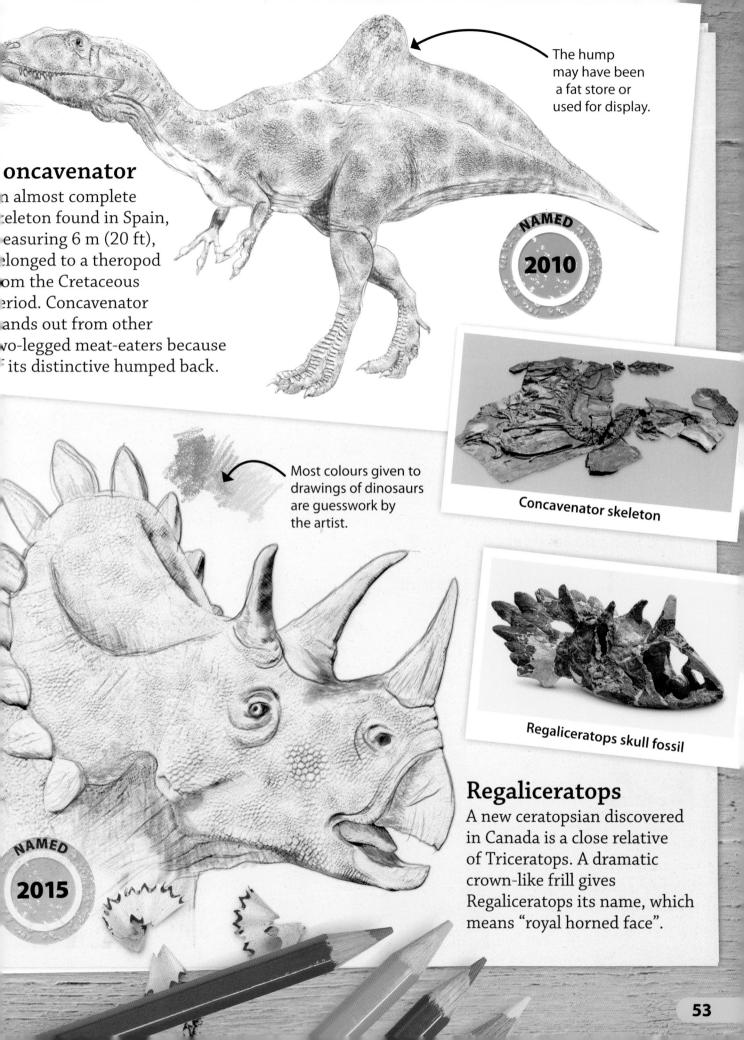

The hump may have been a fat store or used for display.

oncavenator

n almost complete
keleton found in Spain,
easuring 6 m (20 ft),
elonged to a theropod
om the Cretaceous
eriod. Concavenator
ands out from other
vo-legged meat-eaters because
its distinctive humped back.

NAMED
2010

Concavenator skeleton

Most colours given to drawings of dinosaurs are guesswork by the artist.

Regaliceratops skull fossil

NAMED
2015

Regaliceratops

A new ceratopsian discovered in Canada is a close relative of Triceratops. A dramatic crown-like frill gives Regaliceratops its name, which means "royal horned face".

Dinosaur facts and figures

Dinosaurs were a fascinating group of reptiles. Here are some weird and wonderful facts you might not know about them!

TROODON
is thought to have been the most clever dinosaur because it had a large brain compared to its relatively small size.

The **most expensive dinosaur fossil** in the world is the **skeleton of "Sue" the T. rex**, which cost the The Field Museum of Natural History in Chicago, USA, **$8,362,000**!

Compsognathus had a top speed of 64 kph (40 mph), which is faster than an Olympic sprinter

12

is how old the English fossil hunter Mary Anning was when she found the first ichthyosaur, a type of ancient marine reptile.

2,300

The first dinosaur discovery might have been as long as 2,300 years ago, when a Chinese man called Chang Qu wrote about finding some "dragon" bones.

. REX LIVED CLOSER TO US IN TIME THAN IT DID TO **STEGOSAURUS**!

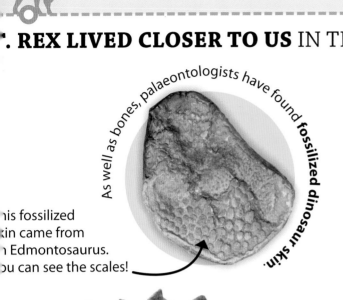

As well as bones, palaeontologists have found **fossilized dinosaur skin.**

his fossilized
kin came from
Edmontosaurus.
ou can see the scales!

In **2006**, a new dinosaur was named **Dracorex hogwartsia**, which means **"dragon king of Hogwarts"**.

A TITANOSAUR

was discovered in Argentina in 2014 that weighed **70 tonnes (77 tons)**, which is the same weight as 10 elephants!

1,000

pecies of dinosaur have been
amed so far.

169 MILLION

years is how long the dinosaurs lived on Earth. Modern humans have only been around for 200,000 years.

Before dinosaurs

By 310 MYA there were reptiles, amphibians, invertebrates, and fish. Trilobites, woodlouse-like sea creatures, died out before the dinosaurs even appeared.

» 235 million years ago

First dinosaurs

The earliest dinosaurs appeared around 235 MYA. Dinosaurs like Eoraptor lived alongside other huge reptiles.

» 130 MYA

Iguanodon
This dinosaur existed for about five million years in the Cretaceous period.

» 140 MYA

First ceratopsians
These horned dinosaurs made their entrance in the Early Cretaceous.

» 155 MYA

First birds
Archaeopteryx was one of the first birds.

» 125 MYA

First flowering plants
The first flowers were small compared to ones today. By 100 MYA many recognizable flowers were blooming, such as magnolias.

» 112 MYA

Spinosaurus
Spinosaurus walked the Earth for five million years in the Cretaceous.

» 100 MYA

First bees
Once flowers had appeared so did flower-loving insects such as bees.

Dinosaurs and us

» 30 MYA

First cats
Early cats were meat-eaters, just like cats today.

Dinosaurs existed for almost 170 million years, but this is just a moment in the 3.8 billion years of life on Earth. A huge range of animals and plants appeared before, alongside, and after them. Once dinosaurs had disappeared, other types of animal, like mammals, took over.

»215 MYA

First mammals
The first hairy mammals, such as Megazostrodon, were small and rat-like.

»195 MYA

First sauropods
Early sauropods were much smaller than their later relatives like Diplodocus, which lived 154 MYA.

»90 MYA

First snakes
Some reptiles lost their limbs and became the first snakes.

»80 MYA

First ants
Insects appeared before the dinosaurs, but ants only arrived near the end of the Cretaceous.

»70 MYA

Tyrannosaurus rex
This king of the reptiles only had four million years on Earth before the dinosaurs became extinct.

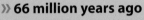

»66 million years ago

Dinosaurs extinct

The end of the Cretaceous saw the extinction of the giant dinosaurs, such as T. rex. Around 70 per cent of all animals and plants were wiped out.

»35 MYA

First dogs
Unlike modern dogs, early dogs had very long tails.

»60 MYA

First primates
The first primates were small and lived in trees.

»7 million years ago

First humans

Seven million years ago there was more than one type of human-like animal. Modern humans didn't appear until as recently as 200,000 years ago.

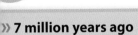

Modern humans

There are now more than seven billion people living on Earth. Humans live on all seven continents and have even made the leap into space! To see into the ancient past we have to look for fossils and other remains of prehistoric animals.

How to say it

This guide will show you how to say each dinosaur's name and what it means. Capital letters mean you should say that part of the name a tiny bit louder.

Albertosaurus
(Al-BERT-oh-SAW-rus)
lizard from Alberta

Allosaurus
(Al-uh-SAW-rus)
different lizard

Alxasaurus
(Al-xa-SAW-rus)
Alxa Desert lizard

Anchiornis
(ANG-kee-OR-niss)
nearby bird

Ankylosaurus
(an-KYE-low-SAW-rus)
fused lizard

Anzu
(an-ZOO)
feathered demon

Apatosaurus
(a-PAT-oh-SAW-rus)
deceptive lizard

Aquilops
(ah-QUILL-ops)
eagle face

Archaeopteryx
(ar-kee-OP-ter-ix)
ancient wing

Argentinosaurus
(AHR-jen-TEEN-uh-SAW-rus)
Argentina lizard

Barosaurus
(BARE-uh-SAW-rus)
heavy lizard

Brachiosaurus
(BRACK-ee-oh-SAW-rus)
armed lizard

Chindesaurus
(CHIN-dee-SAW-rus)
lizard from Chinde Point

Citipati
(sit-ih-PA-tee)
lord of the funeral pyre

Coelophysis
(see-lo-FISE-iss)
hollow form

Compsognathus
(KOMP-SOW-NAY-thus)
pretty jaw

Concavenator
(KON-cav-ee-nah-tor)
predator from Cuenca

Confuciusornis
(KON-FYOO-shi-SOR-nis)
Confucius bird

Cryolophosaurus
(KRIE-ol-lof-oh-SAW-rus)
frozen-crested lizard

Deinonychus
(dye-NON-ik-us)
terrible claw

Diplodocus
(dip-LOD-oh-kus)
double-beamed

Dracorex hogwartsia
(DRAK-o-rex HOG-wart-cia)
dragon king of Hogwarts

Dreadnoughtus
(dread-NOUGHT-iss)
fears nothing

Edmontosaurus
(ed-MONT-oh-SAW-rus)
Edmonton lizard

Einiosaurus
(eye-nee-oh-SAW-rus)
buffalo lizard

Eocursor
(ee-oh-KUHR-sor)
dawn runner

Eoraptor
(ee-oh-RAP-tor)
dawn raptor

Euoplocephalus
(you-op-luh-SEF-uh-lus)
well-armoured lizard

Giganotosaurus
(gi-GAN-oh-toh-SAW-rus)
giant southern lizard

Giraffatitan
(gi-RAF-a-TIE-tan)
giant giraffe